The M
W

# The Mini-Pupillage Workbook

DAVID S. BOYLE

boyle@deanscourt.co.uk

Deans Court Chambers

24 St. John Street

Manchester

M3 4DF

Law Brief Publishing

Published 2019 by Law Brief Publishing,
an imprint of Law Brief Publishing Ltd,
30 The Parks, Minehead, Somerset, TA24 8BT

www.lawbriefpublishing.com

Paperback: 978-1-912687-74-9

*To Paul Garner, David Chart and Iain Morrow:*
*Three long-suffering, non-lawyer, friends who*
*between them have for a hundred years*
*encouraged me to achieve calm self-awareness*
*whilst putting up with my forensic intensity.*

*AND IN MEMORY OF*

*Peter Clark (1940-2019), who, like my dad,*
*encouraged me to solve puzzles.*

# FOREWORD

David and I once tried to persuade a group of students about a point of law (which he kindly recalls on p. 43). It was a debate in the Cambridge Union, as part of a sixth form conference showing more about what a Law degree would be like.

I barely now recall what we were debating, and sadly only a few of the students' faces. But what I do remember vividly is David's passion for helping aspiring lawyers to know about the Law and how to make their way in it. Some years later, the generous portion of his passion that beats for mini-pupils has been distilled and packaged in the volume you now hold.

You can feel David's warmth, his experience, his wisdom and his avuncular charm in every page, even the blank ones (that give you a space for quilting your own thoughts into your particular copy of the book). He offers his views "knowing that they will create debate and making it clear that others will disagree", and it is just that inspiration and openness which will help future students.

He notes that CVs and cover letters should be short but sweet (p. 23), and indeed, like a skeleton argument for a barrister or many first contact situations, "Your covering letter is your first chance to knock on [the door]. It should be crisp, clear and effective. It should reflect both you and the person to whom you are writing. It should show that you have the capacity to grow into a role where you might well be paid by reference to the quality of your written word" (p. 24).

If I were forced (and it would require significant force) to select just two pieces of advice from this book, the first would be that, and the second would be all the contents of Chapter 7 (swiftly followed by Chapter 10!).

Matthew Dyson
Corpus Christi College
25 November 2019

# AUTHOR'S NOTE

This book is not a definitive guide to mini-pupillage or a career in the law, but is a collection of personal offerings, born out of my own 5 mini-pupillages, my pupillage, 23 years in tenancy, 3 formal pupils, 4 informal pupils, 18 mentees, 6 years running the mini-pupillage at Deans Court Chambers (let's call that 1,200 applications, 500 MPs through the door and 350 marked Homeworks™), and 1,000+ mini-pupils, over 100 of whom I have now seen make it to the Bar.

Brian Clough said he wasn't the best manager in the business, but was in the top one. I have no such illusions. This is simply a collection of my original thoughts, honed and polished over the years, and offered in the hope that they provide a stepping stone or catalyst for readers, not the one route to goal.

I believe that any putative barrister should have the capacity for independence of thought. It follows that the reader should feel free to disagree with my offerings. I am more than happy to accept that, but please don't be offended if you do: Being offended doesn't make you right.

So this is what I'd try to tell you on a mini-pupillage with me. You'd have signed a confidentiality agreement before entering chambers, so that we might talk freely. I offer you my views. They are mine and mine alone.

**DSB**
17 November 2019

# ACKNOWLEDGEMENTS

There have been an awful lot of mini-pupils (helpfully supplied by my clerks) who have listened to some of the contents of this book over the last 24 years. The fact that they didn't run screaming from the room has encouraged me to commit these thoughts to writing. You can blame them.

My thanks to Tim Kevan and Garry Wright at Law Brief Publishing for continuing to accede to my desires to avoid 'niche' legal topics and for working on a book in a different format to try to make it as accessible as possible.

My thanks to my wife, Carin, not least for her input into the format of this book, and my son, John. They have patiently provided huge support for which I'm massively grateful. I suspect that they've heard the contents of this book far more often than they, or I, would have liked.

# CONTENTS

# PART THREE – THE MOTIVATIONAL

# INTRODUCTION

Despite the title, this book is aimed at any and every student who is considering a career in law, in whatever role. The ideas set out are designed to make you think in a different way: to take what you've been taught to date and to develop your thought processes to make you a better lawyer. It is, in many ways, about the philosophy of legal practice.

This is, however, as the title suggests, a practical book. It is not designed as a panacea for those seeking work-experience, mini-pupillage, pupillage or a tenancy. It is not a compilation of the received wisdom of ages. It is certainly not gospel.

It is, instead, a reflection of my thinking, my under-standing, and that which I have learned from my first legal work experience in 1988, through my mini-pupillages in 1993, and throughout my time at Deans Court Chambers from 1995. I took my first mini-pupils (two of them!) into a frankly rather difficult conference early in my second six in May 1996. That was an awful idea for which I never really thanked my clerks.

From then on, I was one of the first on the team sheet when it came to "taking the mini-pupil", and in 2010 after agitating for the role, I was appointed Head of

Mini-Pupillage (although HMP normally has different connotations).

I wanted each mini-pupil to have a bespoke experience which would help them make their career decisions, even if they decided not to come to the Bar at all. In the course of meeting literally hundreds of mini-pupils and students the same ideas came out again and again. Certain situations and conversations arose so regularly that kernels of wisdom started to form, and they in turn developed into monologues (some would call them diatribes). Not every mini-pupil received every monologue, although some may have come very close.

This book takes 12 of those monologues and offers them as starting points for the reader in the hope that they can use that insight, and develop their own thoughts and practices accordingly. They fall into 3 broad categories.

Part One offers my thoughts and advice to the individual looking to add experience (and experiences) to their academic achievements. Chapter 1 mirrors a LinkedIn post which had 15,000 views within 3 days and is clearly close to the heart of many students. Chapters 2 and 3 stray into the realm of Personnel

Managers and Careers Advisors, who will doubtless disagree with my analysis. I offer my views knowing that they will create debate and making it clear that others will disagree. Chapter 4 is something so simple that it's tragic that nobody else mentions it.

Part Two is aimed at developing thought processes, irrespective of the area of law in which one might choose to operate. Chapter 5 deals with drivers of behaviour. Chapter 6 is the basis of a lecture which I have delivered several times over the years to students at all levels, deconstructing their learning methods. Chapter 7 is the single most important lesson I can provide, and Chapter 8 gives a personal insight into the role of the barrister in the trial process.

Part Three forms, I suppose, my personal creed. Some barristers are motivated by altruism (and good for them). Some barristers are in it for the money (and have doubtless made more from this job than I ever will). I am an obsessive problem-solver. But with those drivers of our own behaviour come huge responsibilities, and the need to step back and consider what we do and how we treat others is a central part of our professional standing. For those wanting guidance as to what to do and how to behave on a mini-pupillage, I've hidden it in Chapter 10. I hope that my personal views help others.

There are three obvious points about this book which are worth making at this stage:

Firstly, this is a book which is designed to be read, and hopefully more than once.

Secondly, this is a book which is designed to go with you, with a smaller, guide-book, format that will fit in a pocket or a bag. It can be used as an aide memoire both during and after a day spent with lawyers.

Thirdly, this is a book which is designed to be written in. The contents are a starting point, but there are spaces in the text so that the reader can make their own notes of their observations, identifying whether they correlate corroborate or challenge this book. In time, it should provide preparation materials for applications and interviews.

So what's included? Each chapter contains a monologue, an analysis section, a practice section and room for the reader's own notes.

The monologues are in my words[1]. They represent my oral tradition, committed to paper, and I hope that by keeping that original language I can convey my own passion for these topics in a way which might be diluted were I to perfect the language.

These are set pieces that I deliver to students and mini-pupils at an appropriate juncture during the day or so that they might spend with me. Some are offered as advice to people who ask for guidance with applications. Some are only used when a specific situation arises, but each has been delivered hundreds of times, and, like certain passages in the *Iliad*, there is hopefully a sense that these are the core of this narrative, whether the monologue itself is detailed or pithy.

The analysis section is not exhaustive. That's not the purpose of this book. Indeed, in some cases, the analysis is almost otiose, and I have kept it to the bare minimum. It is an expansion of the basic tenet, but in reality it is nothing more than a bridge to allow the reader to step off into their own journey.

---

1  For those wanting authenticity, it's a relatively neutral baritone with some flat Northern vowels, descending into a grumbling bass when I'm trying to push a point (see chapter 4). In the real world, we'd probably be sitting around drinking vast amounts of black coffee.

The practice section is simply signposting in many cases. It gives the reader some further guidance about how they might develop their thinking on a subject. It is not designed to be definitive. It is not a tick box exercise where one gets a certificate at the conclusion, but it offers some further ideas for the direction the reader might take.

The notes section is as important as anything else. These blank spaces are designed for your thoughts, your notes, your doodles. Sometimes I have posed questions and given you space for your answers. Sometimes I have posed the question more than once, so that you can return to the exercise again and again, on each placement you undertake.

I hope that you graffiti this book, that it becomes an old, lived-in, friend to you, and that in years to come you develop your own oral traditions which you might pass on to the next generation with this as an aide memoire.

# How To Use This Book[1]

My recommendation, and it is only that, is to read this book with a pencil in your hand. In due course, you can move to pen, but the first time you read it, use a pencil. Don't use a marker – if this book is doing its job properly, you'll obliterate the whole text.

Pick a chapter. They're all independent. I've ordered them in a way which I think works, but you might have somewhere specific you'd like to start.

Read the monologue. Don't make any notes this first time around. Just listen to it in your head. This is a personal conversation. It just happens to have been reduced to writing so that you can revisit it in due course.

When you get to the end of the monologue, stop. Put your pencil in that page to mark it, and close the book. Listen to it again in your head. Take a few minutes just to let it sink in. Ask yourself questions:

---

1   These ideas mirror those of the late, great chess grandmaster, David Ionovich Bronstein (1924-2006), from his book *The Sorcerer's Apprentice*. I played him some 30 years ago, which (for those remotely interested) gives me a Morphy Number of 4. For those to whom this means nothing, he was a lovely man, whose apparent acceptance of the vicissitudes which he faced was astonishing. Given that this book is about us as people and how we interact with others and the world around us, I have no qualms about namechecking him here. (c.f. Chapter 3)

Does it make sense? Did I know that? Does that change anything? What does this mean?

Formulate those basic ideas in your mind, and then open the book again and reread the monologue from the beginning. Use your pencil to put a mark in the margin next to anything to which you attach particular importance.

Now read the analysis section. See whether it coincides with your thoughts. Revisit the monologue, and your notes. Develop your thoughts, and feel free to make any further notes.

It may be that you want to address the issues raised here and now. That might be why you bought the book. If that's the case, read on, and think about the practice and note sections.

But it might be the case that what you've read will only become relevant once you're sitting in court or in interview, making an application or attending a mini-pupillage, and that's when I hope that you pick up this book once more, refreshing your memory so that you can get the most out of seeing these ideas in practice. Reread chapters 4, 8 and 10 before you go to court. Reread 5, 9 and 11 before you sit in a conference. Reread chapter 1 before and after any given work experience. And reflect on what you then see or do, and make notes, whether in this book or somewhere else, about what you then did and how it might relate, so that you might build up your knowledge and understanding over time.

Most importantly, enjoy this book and your career development. The Bar is not for everybody, and there is no shame in deciding that your particular skill set is better suited to a different role. Many of my mini-pupils had the insight, and were bold enough, to decide that being a barrister was not what they wanted to do. I was delighted that they took that from their time with me. Many of the lessons in this book are of general importance whether you end up working in the law or not, because they relate to how we deal with people. Sometimes we forget how to do that.

# PART ONE

# THE PERSONAL

# Chapter One
## The Four Questions To Answer

**The Monologue:**
You need to answer 4 basic questions for yourself:
1. Do I want to be a barrister, or a solicitor, or something else? And why not the alternatives?
2. In which city would I like to be based? And why not the alternatives?
3. Is there a specific area of law in which I'd like to work? And why not the alternatives?
4. Am I good enough?

**The Analysis:**
The Careers Advisor will tell you that you that if you're doing a Law degree, there are really only two exit strategies – the Solicitor route, or the Bar. In reality, there are a host of jobs in the law, each with different skill sets required. Doing a Law degree does not mean that you'll be a lawyer, any more than doing a degree in Politics makes you a politician. It does, however, give you a particular way of thinking, and of analysing material.

That said, some people are suited to work with the written word, some with oral advocacy, some with people, some with esoteric research. Importantly, there is no one combination which makes an individual a barrister or a solicitor. The skills of a criminal advocate bear little resemblance to drafting a complex multi-party contract. The empathy required when working with injured clients is completely different to the number-crunching that might be required in commercial litigation.

Understanding what you're good at and where you fit in is the crux of your work experience, but you have to understand that it might not cover the precise area of practice in which you're interested, or that the area of law which you find fascinating in your studies is very different in real life. Undertaking work experience, or mini-pupillage, is often about identifying things that you would rather avoid in the long-term. That is not a negative: it's defining your parameters in a far more pragmatic and constructive way.

To put that in context, rather than do 15 criminal mini-pupillages with every set you can find in Cleethorpes, if you see Family work with solicitors in Leeds, Employment with barristers in Birmingham, Commercial with solicitors in London, and Crime with barristers in Liverpool, you will build a portfolio of experience where each placement answers more than one question. Of course, you'll probably end up doing Personal Injury work in Manchester...

**Practice:**
Start by looking at your CV, and looking at the 4 basic questions. Have you thought about any of those questions as either/or questions before, or have you

only ever asked yourself the leading question: Do I want to be a barrister?

Work out a plan for answering those questions. You don't need to visit 4 different cities, but you at least see the difference between London and the provinces.

Put yourself out there. Don't be afraid of rejection. Send out a tranche of applications and see how you get on. If you receive three offers from similar chambers, don't be afraid to say to one of them: "Thank you so much for your offer. I've actually had a very similar offer three weeks ago from someone else and I don't want to waste your time. I'm happy to come and see you, either for the full period you've offered me, or just for a quick chat, because I'd love to get a feel for the place, but I know that there are other people out there who might not have had as many offers as I've received." You might, of course, be missing out on an opportunity, but equally your maturity and self-awareness might count in your favour. The important thing is to have one eye on answering the necessary questions.

Each time that you get an offer, or a rejection, think about what you've gained from that. Even a rejection letter can be used to your advantage. Why did they reject you? Have they offered you feedback? Do I now have a contact name which I didn't have before? Is it worth me repeating my application in the future?

**Your notes:**
Where have I been?
What have I seen?
Who did I see?
What did I learn?
How does this feed back into the 4 questions?

Where have I been?
What have I seen?
Who did I see?
What did I learn?
How does this feed back into the 4 questions?

Where have I been?
What have I seen?
Who did I see?
What did I learn?
How does this feed back into the 4 questions?

Where have I been?
What have I seen?
Who did I see?
What did I learn?
How does this feed back into the 4 questions?

Where have I been?
What have I seen?
Who did I see?
What did I learn?
How does this feed back into the 4 questions?

# CHAPTER TWO
# LETTER WRITING

**The Monologue:**
If you're writing to an individual, start with "Dear Mr Boyle" and sign off with "Yours sincerely".

If you're writing to an organisation, start with Dear Sirs and sign off with "Yours faithfully".

After that, you're on a slippery slope:

"Dear David Boyle" is always wrong, even if I once received an election leaflet bearing that phrase from (supposedly) David Cameron.

"Dear Sir or Madam" suggests that you don't know who I am despite the fact that you're writing to me. It's become fashionable as a supposedly more egalitarian option to Dear Sirs, although the advent of new pronouns will doubtless cause further issues.

"Dear Sir" is better (what with me being a man), but wrong given that you know my name. It sounds respectful, and there's nothing wrong with that *per se* but it's unnecessary.

"Dear Sire" suggests that I run a stud farm. "Dear Sire/Madame" introduces the possibility of a brothel.

"To whom it may concern" is appropriate if you're writing a reference letter which you understand might be shown to currently unidentified people at some point in the future. "To whom it might concern" suggests that it might not. "To whomsoever it might concern" is getting silly, whilst "To whomsoever it might concern within Deans Court Chambers" opens up the possibility that if the reader picks it up on an email whilst out and about it can legitimately be ignored.

After that, things get worse. "Good morning!" It isn't. And I'm reading it in the middle of the night. "Hi!" You probably are. "Hello!" Good-bye.

It sounds picky, and it probably is, but I wouldn't want an otherwise excellent application to be marked down for a simple mistake which could so easily be avoided.

## The Analysis:
Over the years, I have seen dozens of people make the same mistakes with a covering letter when asking for a mini-pupillage or work experience. Letter writing is no longer taught in schools, and the advent of electronic communication means that we no longer have to sit and think before sending off applications. I still write hand-written letters of congratulation when I get the chance. I'm told by their recipients that, in many cases, it's the first hand-written letter that they've ever received. Legible handwriting is a prerequisite in those circumstances.

A good covering letter, or email, is hugely important. It is the first thing that the busy recipient will read. Deciding what belongs in the CV and what belongs in the covering letter is very much up for debate. I tend towards the minimalist CV: The last application that I made consisted of a 2½ page covering letter setting out why I was suitable for the role, my professional CV condensed to a single side of A4, and my testimonials on a second sheet.

The covering letter allows you to explain what you want and how you can be useful to the reader. It does not need to be high flattery or hyperbole about your own merits. It needs to be straight-forward, simple, sensible, and offer the reader the opportunity to contact you if they have any questions.

Telling a lawyer (who is the person to whom you are probably writing at this point) that you are keen, highly motivated, exceptionally intelligent, etc. is unhelpful. Nobody is ever going to write that they are diffident, surly, deeply unpleasant and a bit thick. If you're going to boast about attention to detail, make sure that you've run your letter through a spell-checker and haven't misspelt detail.

So keep it simple: Tell the reader who you are, what you would like to achieve, when you can make yourself available and enclose your CV. Be polite, not effusive, and avoid legalese. I once received an application which began:

"Dear Sire, I write to enquire about the possibility of applying to be considered for a position in your high and honourable Chamber. I am flexible and willing to learn."

It did not improve.

Be wary, however, of simply taking a structure from the internet. Anybody can google "mini-pupillage application letter" and, back in 2013, one particular 'sample' would always come up. Over a six-month period, 45% of all applications received included the phrase "I believe that I possess[1] the essential attributes to succeed at the Bar. I am a confident public speaker, able to work both individually and as part of a team."

45% of candidates there, communally demonstrating that they lacked the capacity for independent thought.

So the advice is this: You are wanting to join a (still very traditional) profession where accuracy and clarity are highly regarded. Your covering letter is your first chance to knock on that door. It should be crisp, clear and effective. It should reflect both you and the person to whom you are writing. It should show that you have the capacity to grow into a role where you

---

1   One candidate wrote "I posses". I made the offer, but pointed out that "posses were gangs of vigilante cowboys."

might well be paid by reference to the quality of your written word.

**Practice:**
Read letters that other people have written. See whether you like their style, or whether it makes sense. Think about why they have expressed themselves in the way they have.

Read about how to write a letter. There are several well-known books on grammar, syntax, punctuation, and style.

Draft your letter on screen first. Think about it before you send it. Check the spelling. Use software to make sure that your writing hits the spot without losing your voice.

Don't be afraid to ask teachers, or tutors, whether you're pitching it at the appropriate level, but be warned that non-lawyers might have a different perception of what is required.

Be prepared to write a bespoke letter on each occasion. Cut and paste is a wonderful function, but not so much if you end up sending an application to Chambers X where you explain why a placement of Chambers Y is your dream job.

Keep a record of the letters you send. Look back at them from time to time to see whether your style is progressing.

**Your notes:**
To whom am I writing?

What am I trying to achieve?

When am I available if picked?

Have I included my CV?

Have I referenced the advert?

Have I spell-checked and grammar-checked it?

Have I included contact details and said that they can contact me if they have any queries?

What would I think if I received this letter?

To whom am I writing?

What am I trying to achieve?

When am I available if picked?

Have I included my CV?

Have I referenced the advert?

Have I spell-checked and grammar-checked it?

Have I included contact details and said that they can contact me if they have any queries?

What would I think if I received this letter?

# CHAPTER THREE
## THE DREADED CV

**The Monologue:**
Several years ago, I took my wife to a restaurant called Frantzen in Stockholm for a big birthday. At the time, it was officially the 11th best restaurant in the world. It offered a 14-course tasting menu. It was very expensive. It was superb.

Some of the things that they did were so simple, yet brilliant. We pulled up outside in a taxi and paused, momentarily, to get our bearings as I paid the driver. My wife's car door was opened by a tall, thin, septuagenarian in a long coat and bowler hat. "Ms B__," he said, "I believe that you're dining with us this evening." With hindsight, they knew that we were booked at 7.45pm and that we were probably the only people to be arriving at that time, but that's not the point – when you have had the idea, it seems effortless.

When we got to the table, and having used the hot towels to wash our hands, steam our faces, and clear our heads from the outside world before starting our meal, I looked at the menu.

It simply read:

Canapé
Appetizer
Sashimi
Signature
Catch of the Day
Rôti
Finish

A separate sheet referenced the contents of the Satio Tempestas, their signature salad made solely with 40+ ingredients from their own garden. And that was it.

Now you can watch their videos on the internet, and it is quite clear that there's a little more to their food than the menu suggests, and when each course was delivered, lovingly, to the table by the staff (all trained sommeliers too from what I could make out), they explained what you were getting, so that you could come to terms with what you were about to eat. But when you read that menu, all that you can feel is anticipation: your interest has been piqued and you want to know more. You will never be disappointed, as long as you get something under each heading.

Imagine, however, how you might feel if every single course was laid out on the menu before you. You would look at it and think: "I like the sound of that, not that, I don't like that. Why would they do that? That looks nice etc." And it would detract from the food, from the experience, from the moment, because there is simply too much information there.

The human brain can only hold a limited amount of information at any given time. Most people can manage 3 pieces of information, maybe 4. That's why we split our telephone numbers into easy to remember blocks. Give the brain too much to process and it will fixate on one or two items to the exclusion of others.

The one lecture that I remember from Bar School was a guest lecture by Michael Beloff QC entitled "Simple Is Persuasive". I don't recall the content, but then I didn't really need to.

The same applies to your CV. If you tell the interviewer everything when you write your CV, what are you going to talk about in the interview? Whether it's true? I once sat through a pupillage interview where they spent 23 minutes going through the CV, line by line, asking if it were true. I expanded on each point in turn to prove that it was, but eventually suggested, politely, that it was all true and they could take me at my word on that.

So your CV should be a teaser, particularly when you're looking for work experience or mini-pupillage. If there's something on there that's especially interesting, highlight it in your covering letter, but move on. Make the reader want to meet you to ask about how you came to be building a house on top of a French mountain in the summer after graduation, or how you missed 2 of your 5 second-year exams 'through illness'. If it's important when you get to interview, you can tell them you had concussion after falling on your head climbing out of the mosh pit at the Guns n' Roses gig at Milton Keynes Bowl when the riot broke out, but isn't that story better told face to face rather than set out in gory detail on the face of the CV?

So when you write your CV, be honest, but keep a little back for the reveal. Flirt (innocently!) with your reader, so they want to know more, not less, about you.

**The Analysis:**
Everybody has their own thoughts about what a mini-pupillage CV should have on it, how long it should be, what order things should be in, whether there should be a covering letter, what should be in the letter rather than the CV, etc.

There are books written about the art of the CV. People have made a career out of it. Psychologists, and Personnel Managers, and Recruitment Consultants, and Barristers, all have their views on how you should sell yourself.

But this is about getting work experience, rather than a job *per se*. Chambers may only have a limited number of placements available, and some will assess their mini-pupils with the intention of deciding whether they should progress to a more formal pupillage application, but many see mini-pupillage as being about the student getting relevant experience, hopefully positive, so that they might be inspired in their choice of career (whether at the Bar or otherwise) and have fond memories of their time in Bolton Crown Court, or wherever the diary takes them. The point is that a mini-pupillage might only be for a couple of days or a week, and that means that there is less at stake for Chambers in deciding who they might take on.

With that in mind, you can acknowledge that there might be gaps in your CV. After all, that's why you're doing the work experience in the first place. Identify what you've done to date, and what you'd like to gain from the experience (as *per* Chapter 1). Explain your plan in your covering letter: It's compelling, it shows you can approach things analytically, and it shows an understanding of both the bigger picture and the finer detail.

But most of all, own your CV. There is no point in pretending to be something that you're not. Improving your A-level results to try to gain work experience, particularly in a profession where integrity is every-thing, is mind-blowingly stupid. Being dishonest at that early stage will kill your career stone-dead. Even if you're only asking for a 3-day place-ment, the chances are that you'll be called on it. After all, the people looking at your CV spend their entire lives looking for inaccuracies, inconsistencies, and lies.

So keep your CV simple, straight-forward and honest. You're at an early stage of your career, and you'll have less to put on there. Your exam results are probably more important than other aspects, whilst if you're 20 years down the line, your life experience and work experience is probably more relevant than that B you got in Home Economics at GCSE.

If, however, you have something worthwhile in your application, whether decent exam results, or some extra-curricular activities, or, absent either, a really good reason why you would like a mini-pupillage, say so, either on the face of the CV, or in the covering letter.

Bear in mind that a CV can do more harm than good. Spelling mistakes, or a general lack of proof-reading are a big No, as is an unjustified and over-inflated sell of meaningless 'qualities' which are, in fact, ubiquitous, particularly in the cohort of applicants which you hope to join. Claiming that you are "academically exceptional" with BDE at A-level is a reckless boast given the likely level of intellect and education of the person reading the document (and bear in mind that you can probably look them up online before you send it). Understand the sort of person who will be reading what you write.

Against that background, back in 2010, I received an application for a first mini-pupillage, relying on a CV which referenced a DDD at B-Tech as "equivalent to A-level". Whilst it has become a more common qualification, it was the first time I had seen it on a CV for mini-pupillage, so I looked it up and discovered that it was, in fact, a triple distinction: a simple point which the applicant hadn't thought to mention. It seemed obvious to them, because they knew that a D at B-Tech was a top mark, and it never occurred that it might be compared to a D at A-level. I suspect that many wouldn't have made the effort to look it up.

Yes, I made an offer. Yes, we tweaked the CV. Yes, we're still in touch nearly a decade later. Yes, I'm hugely proud of everything they have achieved since. They put in all the hard work: all I did was strip back the CV to a simple framework from which to build, and help them to explain in their covering letter who they were, how they got to where they were, and where they wanted to go next. And they did.

Equally, another applicant said on their CV that they had 3 A-levels (A* to D). When I asked what they actually were, the grades were A*AD. They'd elected to study locally for financial reasons and had gone to the "new university" because that's where their school friends had gone, despite having the grades to study elsewhere. The Careers Advisor had suggested to the group that given that most of them had CCD or similar, obfuscation was the order of the day. A modest tweak later and, again, I am delighted with their ongoing achievements.

Early in 2019, I made an application which required a covering letter (no more than 4 pages) and a CV. My covering letter ran to 3 pages. For the first time in 25 years, had to write my CV. It ran to one page. It sufficed.

**Practice:**
Be honest with yourself and your reader.

Ask what you're hoping to achieve with the application.

Consider the selling points on your CV and how you can convey them simply.

Are there any negative issues to be dealt with? Can I ignore them? Can I explain them? Do I want to give a bare comment which can be picked up at interview? Can I nevertheless own that issue? Don't waste space on the face of the CV, cover it in the letter.

Make your CV a pleasure to read. Keep it simple. Feel free to use bold for headings. Use a sensible font (and yes, I know that serif fonts are old hat and the trend is for sans serif fonts like Arial, but ask yourself whether reading this book in Garamond is working for you).

Declutter your CV. Your 15-metre breaststroke certificate when you were 6 years old isn't relevant any more, nor is your hobby of socialising. If you've no hobbies, focus on your academics, or your experiences to date. If you have none of the traditional selling points, explain why you nevertheless would like to experience the Bar. You'll be pleasantly surprised.

Set out the salient matters, and be prepared to flirt with the reader. If you've undertaken mini-pupillages previously, distil them to the purest form that you can whilst retaining a sense that each was different from the rest. In other words, if you've done 4 criminal mini-pupillages, you might want to emphasise that you saw a sexual offence one week, a dishonesty case the next, motoring offences the next, etc. If you're following the advice in Chapter 1, you'll be able to say: "Birmingham, Mini-pupillage, Employment Law" and leave it at that. Let them ask you about it, as and when it becomes relevant.

Before sending off your CV, with your beautifully crafted covering letter, step back and read it as if you were receiving it. Better still, get somebody else to look it over. Are there any typos? Does it tell me enough about you to make me want more information? Does it invite instant consignment to the bin? The art of advocacy starts early: Simple is Persuasive.

**Your notes:**
What information do I want to include in my CV?

What gaps am I happy to identify on my CV, so that I can justify trying to fill them?

What belongs in the CV and what in the covering letter?

Do I need to update my CV yet? (Hint: Yes. Each and every time.)

Can I make it simpler?

## Chapter Four
## Breathe

**The Monologue:**
Breathe in. Now say: "My name is ..."
Now do it again, but this time, when you've taken that deep breath, and without taking another breath, recite the alphabet before saying "My name is…"
Hard, isn't it?
Now take that breath again, and say "My name is…"

**The Analysis:**
Breathing is not something that we are habitually taught at school or college. Unless you're in the choir, or debating society, it's presumed that you can breathe in and out and will continue to do so, but as a barrister, your voice, whether in court, over the telephone, or in conference with a client, is one of your primary tools. It's critical that you think about it, hone it, and use it.

When we forget to breathe in, we run out of air, we sound panicked, and our volume levels die away. By breathing in before we speak, we give ourselves a split second to think and a full set of lungs with which to deliver our point, and we potentially drop our voices very slightly.

That last point is an interesting one, because various papers over the years[1] suggest that the listener perceives the lower voice as more authoritative, stronger and more trustworthy. Margaret Thatcher famously took voice lessons and is said to have dropped her speaking voice by 60Hz.

So few of my mini-pupils have done any voice work before meeting me. It's just not done any more. Teachers don't tell students to drop their voices – they tell them to speak up – and it is undoubtedly easier for some than others, but simply remembering to breathe in will do wonders for your spoken advocacy.

Despite my physical size, my 'personal' speaking voice is probably a low tenor, dropping into baritone when speaking to clients, talking on the phone, or addressing a district judge. That drops yet further with each level of the judiciary, so by the time I'm in

---

1    "*Sounds like a winner: voice pitch influences perception of leadership capacity in both men and women*", Klofstad, Anderson and Peters, Royal Society, 2012,

"*Listen, follow me: Dynamic vocal signals of dominance predict emergent social rank in humans*", Cheng, Tracy, Ho and Henrich, Journal of Experimental Psychology, 2016

the Court of Appeal, I can't help myself – there's an element of treacle somehow added to the mix.

I do have a voice even lower than my Court of Appeal voice, but I have only found it once: Some years ago, I was asked to take part in a debate at the Cambridge Union. It was the first debate that I'd ever attended sober, and with a last-minute drop-out, I found myself opening the debate, seconded by Dr Matt Dyson, then of Trinity College, Cambridge, and now a Fellow of Corpus Christi, Oxford. He'd had a whole 90 minutes to find his dinner jacket and prepare, so I was sent in to bat first. On the other side of the chamber were two undergraduates, who had just represented the University in a trans-Atlantic debate and were finalists in the European Debating Championships (one was the overall winner). The two hundred or so students in the audience sat, eagerly awaiting intellectual battle on a subject (Anonymity for those accused of sexual offences) about which my years in the job had taught me nothing.

I reached the lectern and laid out my arguments, loving the acoustics of the room but with no huge certainty in the correctness of my content. Having spoken for my allotted time, I returned to my seat, expecting a perfunctory nod from my second, who made my day by leaning across and asking "Could you record my bedtime stories in that voice?"

**Practice**
It's an easy thing to do, either with a friend or on your own. As a child, given lines in a school play, my dad had me stand at the top of the stairs and speak to him as he stood by the front door, just to get used to pushing out my voice. These days, I find a quiet room or space and start next to the other person, holding a normal conversation about whatever comes to mind.

You can then start to move about the room, putting distance between you, so that to continue the conversation you have to push your voices ever so slightly. When you're 20 metres apart, to converse without shouting means that you'll end up breathing slightly more deeply to give that vocal power, gently letting your voice roll out to the listener.

If you're on your own, stand in front of a mirror and talk to yourself. Your listener (the reflection) is, perhaps, a metre away. Now take a step back, and you're 2 metres away. Keep talking to that reflection as you gradually put more distance between you and the mirror, with each step effectively counting double to the distance over which you're speaking.

**Your notes:**
Can you tell the difference when you breathe? What's happening?

Where are you speaking from? Diaphragm? Throat?

What works for you?

Can you repeat it? How?

When do you use different voices? And why?




Can you still go up as well as down? Can you control it?

# PART TWO

# THE PROFESSIONAL

# CHAPTER FIVE
## RULES OF THREE

**The Monologue:**
*The rule of three for claimants[1]:*
When you're representing a claimant, you want to get them as much as possible, as quickly as possible, with as little risk as possible, but they cannot have all three.

*The rule of three for defendants[2]:*
Defendants fight a case to trial for one of three reasons: To discourage the next claim, to resolve irreconcilable differences in the instant case, and a failure to appreciate that the case does not fall into one of the other two categories.[3]

**The Analysis:**
Understanding the drivers of behaviour for your clients (or the other side) is a critical aspect of law in the real world. We are, after all, trying to resolve problematic situations. The analysis set out above is

---

1   Invariably demonstrated by holding up the thumb, index and middle fingers of the left hand at right angles to each other and using the index finger of the right hand to draw a clockwise circle in the air above the fingertips.

2   As above, using right hand.

3   "The solicitors hate each other" is, in fact, a combination of all three.

obviously formulated in the context of civil claims for damages, but can be applied to family law, criminal law and the like:

In crime, you substitute the defendant into the claimant analysis: He wants the best result, as quickly as possible, with as little risk as possible. In reality, the Crown is probably in the same boat, although their starting point will be that of the defendant in the original rule: They want to discourage future criminal conduct, they can't agree to a plea bargain on the basis offered, or they've not set their minds to what they are trying to achieve.

In family, the sides are more evenly balanced, and discouraging the next litigation may not be at the forefront of people's minds, but balancing those factors will give real guidance when you need to stop, step back and assess your options.

In a civil context, the rule of three for claimants is astonishingly useful. Whenever you talk to a client, address those three issues. Never be blasé about the time that people have to wait to resolve their case. Never underestimate the importance of resolution and being able to move on with life. Talk freely about the amounts of money on offer, but balance them against other factors, and encourage clients to tell you about their worries. Bear in mind that for most clients, the amount on offer is hugely in excess of any single lump sum they have ever seen before, or will again: a terrifying prospect.

What is vital is that one understands what is meant by the word risk. It is not merely the risk of losing and getting nothing, or failing to beat an offer. Whilst the word has negative connotations, risk is simply an element of uncertainty. Further evidence might clarify the future medical position for good or ill, but it reduces the risk, because the parties can be more certain of the outcome.

Sometimes a decision has to be made at a point in time when the evidence is unclear. What is the effect of getting another scan? It might delay matters. It might show long-term deterioration which means that the case is worth more, or a lack of degenerative change which means that the case is worth less (albeit that that might be better news for the injured claimant). That is the 'risk' which has to be factored into the assessment, but for anybody advising a client in whatever field of law, this starting point, with its visual reminder, remains an immensely useful tool.

**Practice:**
Consider a case report, or a set of papers, or a problem question with the rules of three in mind.

Think about what might motivate a client. Watch how a lawyer deals with the issues in the case. Rarely will they be so express about the three aspects which are relevant, but see if you can recognise them when they come along.

**Your notes:**
What sort of case was it?
What was at stake?
What was the timescale?
What were the risks?
How could they be balanced up?
Why was the other side acting in that way?

What sort of case was it?
What was at stake?
What was the timescale?
What were the risks?
How could they be balanced up?
Why was the other side acting in that way?

What sort of case was it?
What was at stake?
What was the timescale?
What were the risks?
How could they be balanced up?
Why was the other side acting in that way?

What sort of case was it?
What was at stake?
What was the timescale?
What were the risks?
How could they be balanced up?
Why was the other side acting in that way?

# CHAPTER SIX
## PROBLEMS WITH PROBLEMS

**The Monologue:**
When you open your exam paper, there's a natural tendency to look for the problem questions. Faced with Q1: "Bob finds a £50 note on the platform at the train station…" or Q2: "Property is theft for the purpose of the 1968 Act. Discuss", it is a bold student who eschews Bob and his adventures in favour of the more esoteric essay. We believe, as students, that problem questions reflect the real world, and that if we can answer those questions in the exam paper, that will prepare us for life at the Bar.

There are, however, 4 problems with problems.

The first problem is that the problem question in the exam, or in the tutorial, or the homework, is on the syllabus. In the real world, there's no syllabus.

The second problem is that all of the information required to answer the problem question is contained in the problem. In the real world, things don't always work that way.

The third issue is, perhaps, less obvious. There's never a conflict of evidence in the problem question. We learn our law by looking at the statutes (which have no facts) and the decided cases (which tend to be appellate decisions, and thus have a decided set of facts to which the courts apply the law). In the real world, even the simplest accident might have two versions of events. Bob may not have 'found' his £50 note. Fred might say that it was his £50 note which had just been knocked out of his hand and he stood admiring it.

Finally, when answering a problem question, the student is entitled to accept the veracity of the examiner. Bob found a £50 note. It wasn't a forgery. It wasn't a £20 where he's claiming it was a £50. He did, in fact, find it. In the real world, everybody lies. That might be a little harsh, but everybody has their own perception of the truth, and just because your client tells you something, you don't have to accept it uncritically.

A simple question before continuing: I drive a red car. What colour car do I drive?

Answer: _____

A white one. Just because I said it, and said it convincingly, and was wearing a suit and tie, doesn't make it true.

All of that means that whilst in the confines of the exam, you can answer the question with confidence, because you know all the facts, there's no grey area to be explored in terms of your client's honesty, or the other side's version of events, and it's on the syllabus.

In the real world, however, you can have a client who's not being truthful, an opposing witness (who may or may not be truthful), missing evidence (including things that we may not even realise that we're missing) and there's no syllabus – the scope for different areas of law to collide is enormous.

Don't kid yourself that answering the problem questions in the exam is the be all and end all.

**The Analysis:**
This lesson isn't (just) about realigning your perception of the import of your studies: It's about ensuring that you have street smarts when dealing with the cases which you will face if you decide to work in law, or any other area. The data that you receive, whether from a client, from a document, or even from your own senses, may not be true. Your source might be

corrupted. There might be another version of events (or several). There is no guarantee that only one area of law might be involved.

By having those 4 problems with problems in the back of your mind, you can assess the information before you with a far more critical eye. As a lawyer (whether as a solicitor or barrister) the client is coming to you because they want advice, or a new take on the situation. They want to know what the future might hold, and what the risks might be. They want your take on the Rules of Three, but how can you assess risk if you don't understand the potential flaws in the evidential foundation?

One important aspect is the idea of fuzzy logic. In practical terms, it is important not to think of things in absolute terms. If a witness says that car A was doing 30mph and car B, coming in the opposite direction was also doing 30mph, the obvious conclusion is that they will collide at a combined speed of 60mph, but even the honest witness is guessing, so those speeds might be as low as, say, 20mph (combined speed 40mph) or as high as 40mph (combined speed 80mph). In reality, he might be a little high with one car, and a little low with the other, and the combined speed is still likely to be in the region of 60mph, but you've allowed for the possibility of error in your analysis.

Similarly another witness might have Car A doing 50mph, whilst Car B is only doing 20mph. You can feed that additional information into the melting pot. Gradually you get a better picture, but there's no guarantee that it will ever be unequivocal. Ultimately, a judge has to decide a civil case on the balance of probabilities, having regard to all the evidence. You might be able to influence that, but the important thing is to stay flexible in your thinking, assessing and reassessing the merits of the evidence available to you, and letting the case coalesce, so that you can look at the patterns which emerge and try to foresee where they will lead.

Ultimately, one has to practice and keep practicing, so that this sort of (potentially self-destructive) analysis becomes second nature. If you can learn to see those patterns, you learn how to cut across problems and avoid those outcomes.

**Practice:**
So how do we identify these problems? It's important to bear in mind that they are not going to occur in every case, and where they do occur it might only be in respect of one small issue.

The important thing is to be aware of the problems, even if only at a subconscious level. In the early days, however, it is worth reading your papers, or listening to your client, and expressly considering the 4 points. Have a note in the front of your notebook, and cross-reference it frequently. If you get the chance, do it next time you have a problem question posed in the course of your studies, and imagine what might go wrong in the real world were that a real case. Think about how you might detect the problem and address it or avoid it.

Gradually, these thoughts become second nature, but never be afraid to stop and reassess your case, or that of your opponent, by reference to the 4 problems: It may well show you the best outcome. Use that analysis not only whilst you're reading your papers, but when you get to the end of them too. It won't take a minute, but it will save you huge time in the long run.

**Your notes:**
What are we looking at? Which area of law? What type of litigation? What is the nominal syllabus for this problem? Are we going to go beyond that?

What do we know? What do we not know? What might we want to know, or need to know? How do I get that information?

What does the other side say about this issue? Which version is more credible? Why? What are the strengths of my evidence? What about their strengths? Are there issues that I need to think about in terms of showing a lack of credibility?

How does my client's version of events hang together? Is there objective evidence to support or undermine his case? What would change my mind?

What are we looking at? Which area of law? What type of litigation? What is the nominal syllabus for this problem? Are we going to go beyond that?

What do we know? What do we not know? What might we want to know, or need to know? How do I get that information?

What does the other side say about this issue? Which version is more credible? Why? What are the strengths of my evidence? What about their strengths? Are there issues that I need to think about in terms of showing a lack of credibility?

How does my client's version of events hang together? Is there objective evidence to support or undermine his case? What would change my mind?

What are we looking at? Which area of law? What type of litigation? What is the nominal syllabus for this problem? Are we going to go beyond that?

What do we know? What do we not know? What might we want to know, or need to know? How do I get that information?

What does the other side say about this issue? Which version is more credible? Why? What are the strengths of my evidence? What about their strengths? Are there issues that I need to think about in terms of showing a lack of credibility?

How does my client's version of events hang together? Is there objective evidence to support or undermine his case? What would change my mind?

What are we looking at? Which area of law? What type of litigation? What is the nominal syllabus for this problem? Are we going to go beyond that?

What do we know? What do we not know? What might we want to know, or need to know? How do I get that information?

What does the other side say about this issue? Which version is more credible? Why? What are the strengths of my evidence? What about their strengths? Are there issues that I need to think about in terms of showing a lack of credibility?

How does my client's version of events hang together? Is there objective evidence to support or undermine his case? What would change my mind?

What are we looking at? Which area of law? What type of litigation? What is the nominal syllabus for this problem? Are we going to go beyond that?

What do we know? What do we not know? What might we want to know, or need to know? How do I get that information?

What does the other side say about this issue? Which version is more credible? Why? What are the strengths of my evidence? What about their strengths? Are there issues that I need to think about in terms of showing a lack of credibility?

How does my client's version of events hang together? Is there objective evidence to support or undermine his case? What would change my mind?

# CHAPTER SEVEN
## PROBLEM SOLVING

**The Monologue:**
When a claimant in a personal injury action is partly at fault for his injuries, his damages can be reduced to reflect his contributory negligence. If he's found to be 20% at fault, he gets 80% of his damages: it's not rocket science. If there's more than one defendant to blame, that 20% comes off the top, before their shares are determined.

In deciding the extent of a claimant's contributory negligence, we look at two separate issues: the extent to which the claimant's conduct was blameworthy ("moral turpitude"[1]) and the relative effect of that blameworthiness in the context of the accident ("causative potency").

A classic case comes about when a passenger in a car chooses not to wear a seatbelt. The moral turpitude of not wearing a seatbelt is the same whatever the consequences, but the consequences can be very different.

The leading case on seatbelts is *Froom v Butcher*[2] where Lord Denning set out guidance which, whilst

---

1 And to be clear, if I ever have a backing band, they are absolutely going to be called "The Moral Turpitudes".

occasionally challenged, is still used today, even though the case predates the mandatory use of seatbelts. Lord Denning identified three[3] scenarios which arise when somebody fails to wear a seatbelt:

In some cases, wearing a seatbelt would avoid any significant injury at all. In those cases, the claimant's negligence has had a substantial effect and the damages are reduced by 25%.

In the second category, the injured person would still have been injured, but not to the same extent. In those cases, the reduction is 15%.

In the third category, the fact that the claimant wasn't wearing a seatbelt has no effect on the injuries. With causative potency at 0%, so too is the reduction for contributory negligence.[4]

---

2   [1976] 1 QB 286

3   There are four.

4   The nominal fourth category is the circumstances where not wearing a seatbelt actually avoids more serious injury: the claimant is, for instance, thrown out of the car before it goes off the cliff. The claimant does not get negative contributory negligence points and an enhanced award!

With that all in mind, solve this problem:

A is driving a car at or about the speed limit in a 30mph zone with B and C sitting in the rear offside and rear nearside seats respectively. None of them is wearing a seatbelt. D is driving a similar car in the opposite direction, at high speed, with E as his front seat passenger. Neither of them is wearing a seatbelt either.

D drives on to the wrong side of the road and there is a head-on collision, with A's car propelled backwards and spun around.

A, C and E are killed, whilst B and D suffer multiple, but non-life threatening, injuries. You are instructed by A's family to pursue a claim against D, who was clearly driving too fast and on the wrong side of the road, but his insurers have taken the point that A was negligent in not wearing a seatbelt. Photographs of the two badly damaged cars show extensive damage to the front of both vehicles consistent in each case with an impact with a brick wall at approximately 40mph.

To keep it simple, it's a multiple choice: Is the appropriate reduction for A's failure to wear a seatbelt:

A.  25%

B.  15%

C.  0%

D.  Other (please specify)

E.  Other (please specify)?

Before continuing, make a note of your thoughts here...

Answer: _____

If you answered A, you need to go back and read *Froom v Butcher*. A(25%) represents the possibility that the driver, had he been wearing a seatbelt, would have been uninjured, in what was clearly a serious accident.

About 10% answer B(15%). The vast majority, after some consideration, plump for C(0%).

Be honest with yourself here. You went for B or C didn't you? You may have flirted with some idea about the unrestrained rear passenger being to blame (before remembering that you take the Claimant's fault off the top before dividing blame between the other people), or you thought about the angle of impact, or how far the car was spun, but ultimately, you went for B (not dead) or C (dead anyway). There are no other answers.

And yet there are. Your first thought was "Why am I being offered not one, but two, 'Other (please specify)' options?" And then you went back to deciding whether A would have lived or died.

Is that a question of law? No it's not. Is that a question of fact? Yes? Are you sure? Because it's actually a counter-factual, isn't it? What would have happened in the alternative reality where A wore a seatbelt?

And that is not a question of fact, but a question of opinion. And who can give evidence of opinion? An expert. And what are you and I not for these purposes? Experts.

So the correct answer is, in fact, D: "*I don't know.*"

Pause there. If you're reading this book, you are well into your second decade of education. You're intelligent and educated. "I don't know" has never been a good answer to anything. What's 1+1? I don't know. Did you eat the last biscuit? I don't know. Did you flick your sister's ear when I wasn't looking? I don't know.

So we take all those factors and we train to be lawyers: experts in answering questions. We hope that people will pay us a great deal of money to answer their questions. We convince ourselves that not only might we answer questions, but that we can and should. We fall into the second 'problem with problems' from the previous chapter, and we think that we have a clear understanding of the answer, whilst forgetting that we don't have all of the information.

Pause again. "*I don't know.*" It changes the way that you think about any question. Having it as an answer opens your mind to the possibility that what you've been told might not be correct. It forces you to consider whether you have all of the information, or whether there's another side to the story, or whether you should even be answering this particular question in the first place.

So, going back to our question, both sides go away and get an expert. A seatbelt expert. Not, perhaps, the obvious choice on a school careers evening. As it happens, the two experts are particularly eminent in their field, and they produce detailed, well-reasoned, reports, after which they discuss the case and produce a joint report, setting out their areas of agreement and disagreement.

In fact, they agree that, had A worn a seatbelt, then on the balance of probability, he would have survived the head on impact. Did you say B(15%)?

He'd have survived, right up until the unrestrained passenger hit the back of his seat. And then they can't agree. One says 51:49 that he would have survived, whilst the other says 51:49 that, unfortunately, he would have died in any event. Each acknowledges that it is on a knife edge. Each acknowledges that the other might well be right. Neither would fall out with the opposing point of view. We still don't know.

What we have here, then, is a real-world Schrödinger's Cat. In 1935, Erwin Schrödinger created a thought experiment involving a cat in a box with a bottle of poison which would be released when a radioactive material decays. The idea is that until the box is opened, we know not whether the cat is alive or dead.[5]

The same applies to our problem. If we go to court, the judge has to answer the question, and is stuck with A, B or C as his answers. As lawyers, of course, we can choose not to go to court. We can settle in advance. We can compromise. We can apply our rule of three for claimants.

And in a case where we have no idea which way the decision will go in court, we are left with an analysis which is that there's approximately a 50% chance of B(15%) and a 50% chance of C(0%), the actual answer, in the real world is: E: A sensible compromise of, as it happens, 7.5%.

There we have it. Lord Denning says that the answer is A, B or C but I offer two further answers: *"I don't know"*, and *"Is there an acceptable compromise?"*

---

5   Indeed, Schrödinger concluded that it was both.

Understanding that is, perhaps, the most important lesson that I can teach. It should change the way that you think… about everything.

**The Analysis:**
This is arguably the single most important advice that I can offer. Executed properly, it will change the shape of your entire thinking. Imagine: When somebody makes to toss a coin and asks you "Heads or Tails?" you simply guess, based on gut reaction, habit, or some other non-scientific method. If you're asked "How is it going to land?" you start to think before you give your answer, not because you're being asked a different question, but because the context is slightly different – you're being asked to make a judgment call, not just give a random response. You start to think about what you know: Is the coin face up or down? Is he going to throw it, spin it, drop it? Is it a biased coin? Do we know what happened last time? Is it a double-headed coin? All of those questions become relevant, because now, because of the way in which the question was asked, we really want to get it right.

What is being suggested here is a different mind-set, which flows from the previous chapter. In time, we learn to challenge what we're told and to challenge whether we have the right information, all on a subconscious level, but part of the training process is to develop that sub-conscious objectivity by, in the first instance, doing it consciously. When a question is asked, think about whether it's within your remit. Some people have the over-confidence to try to answer anything. Some people are under-confident and want every piece of information checked and double-checked. Sometimes you have to acknowledge that you're having to make an educated guess on the information before you, even if that information is potentially sub-optimal. There is a need to balance knowledge and certainty on the one hand, and the need for a decision on the other, which brings us back to chapter 5.

Developing that reservoir of knowledge and experience will allow you to hone this particular skill. You will learn to judge when you need more information and when you can tell a client: "Well nothing's certain, but based on x, y and z, my view is this…"

**Practice:**
In the short term, simply place "*I don't know*" on your drop-down multiple-choice list of possible answers. Don't put it at the top: it will paralyse you in your thinking about the information before you. Put it at the bottom, after all of the other answers that you can

identify. Use it as a check. Being a barrister is not the same as being a solicitor, or most other professions, because there isn't the same sort of peer review that we see elsewhere. Often, you are the peer reviewer of your solicitor's work, and they've come to you for advice. No matter how experienced and competent your solicitor, if they weren't preconditioned or predisposed to accept your advice, they probably wouldn't have come to you in the first place, so there is a real need for a self-imposed safety net. Challenging your opinion before you give it is often the only way.

In the short term, just stop. Look at the ceiling for a second. Ask yourself "Can I answer this question with what I've got, given who I am?"

This time around, I have given one set of notes, because this is a question that needs to be asked so often that you'd fill a book in a week. Use the notes section to consider and record points that you might use to trigger this response in how you think.

**Your notes:**
What's the question?

Who should answer it?

What possible answers might there be?

What do I know?

What should I know but don't know?

What have I not thought about yet?

How sound is my information?

What else do I need to think about before giving the answer?

What would I ask somebody further up the food chain to check before committing myself to this answer?

How sure am I of my answer?

# CHAPTER EIGHT
## THE BALANCE OF POWER

**The Monologue:**
When a witness is being cross-examined by a barrister, there are four factors in play.

1.  The barrister is normally (but not always), more intelligent and/or educated, than the witness. That's not the witness's fault: it's a reality that few people make it to the Bar, and those who do are likely to have those qualities.

2.  The barrister is in his domain. The witness simply doesn't have the experience of the court, of the process, or even of speaking in public.

3.  The barrister is asking the questions. He controls the dialogue, the content, the structure and the tempo.

And against that, there is:

4.  The truth. The barrister doesn't have a dog in that fight. He does not give evidence. He wasn't a witness to events. He is a cipher for his client's case. Here, and only here, does the witness expect to have the advantage.

Which means that my advice to a client before going to court is simple: "The division of labour is that I do the worrying, and you tell the truth. You pay me to do the worrying, and I'm trained for it. I can't tell the truth for you – that's your job, but there's no point in worrying when you can't do anything about it."

Of course, that opens up the interesting question of what would happen were I ever required to give evidence. If factors 1 and 2 are no longer in play, it would become a direct competition between the barrister's grasp of factor 3 and the strength of the evidence.

**The Analysis:**
Cross-examination does not come naturally to most people. It is all too easy to put your case without belief, and without putting the witness's evidence under the microscope. There is no point in asking highly leading questions if the witness is so weak that an answer in your favour looks as if they're just saying yes to make you stop.

**Practice:**
Understanding the dynamic between the barrister and the witness in these terms gives you scope to think about how you might cross-examine. Would you be aggressive and forceful, or tease the answer out carefully? Would you lead or would you ask an open question, even in cross-examination, because you know that they cannot answer it? Would you ask questions to destroy the witness's credibility

completely, or are there pieces of evidence which you'd like to keep intact?

Those are all questions which you can ask yourself when listening to cross-examination. Think about those answers: are they true?

If you get the chance to see a statement before cross-examination, make a note of the topics that you'd want to cover, and any specific points. Think about the order in which you'd approach those topics. Compare your order and your questions to the questions that are actually asked. Think why the barrister chose to ask the questions in the order that they did, and if you get the chance, ask.

Listen to the barrister's speaking voice. Think back to the lessons in chapter 4 and see whether they are actually applying them in real life. Take the bits which you think you can use and make a note. Work out what to avoid.

**Your notes:**
Who did I see?
What was the purpose of the cross-examination?
What methods did the barrister use?
Which methods worked?
Would I have done it the same way? If not, what would I have done differently?

Who did I see?
What was the purpose of the cross-examination?
What methods did the barrister use?
Which methods worked?
Would I have done it the same way? If not, what would I have done differently?

Who did I see?
What was the purpose of the cross-examination?
What methods did the barrister use?
Which methods worked?
Would I have done it the same way? If not, what would I have done differently?

Who did I see?
What was the purpose of the cross-examination?
What methods did the barrister use?
Which methods worked?
Would I have done it the same way? If not, what would I have done differently?

Who did I see?
What was the purpose of the cross-examination?
What methods did the barrister use?
Which methods worked?
Would I have done it the same way? If not, what would I have done differently?

Who did I see?
What was the purpose of the cross-examination?
What methods did the barrister use?
Which methods worked?
Would I have done it the same way? If not, what would I have done differently?

# PART THREE

# THE MOTIVATIONAL

## CHAPTER NINE
## IMPORTANCE TO CLIENT

**The Monologue:**
Most people get married more often than they go to court. And unless you've got a thing for being married by an Elvis-impersonator in some 24-hour Las Vegas wedding parlor *(sic)*, you'd probably want to meet the officiant first. The same applies to your barrister. You want them to be just right. They're your champion. They are going to go into court and fight for you and your interests.

It's like King Arthur and the Round Table. The knights are all different characters. Arthur's in charge, but he's not really doing much questing. Lancelot's the King's champion and the best fighter, but he's off spending a little too much time with Guinevere. Mordred's off plotting, and nobody likes him. Galahad's off questing for the Holy Grail with Percival. Bedivere, Geraint, Gaheris and Gawain (and I always had a soft spot for Gawain) are busy getting stuck in to whatever problems arise but are they destined for greatness in the same way as, say, Galahad?

Each of them is very different – each has strengths and weaknesses – but these are knights: they are strong, wily, forthright, devious, noble, and their job is to stand up and put themselves in the way of trouble. And that's your job. You're the client's hope, and that responsibility is, right here and now, on your shoulders and yours alone. That's how important you are to your client.

## The Analysis:

Being a barrister is a really difficult job. People think that it's difficult to become a barrister, but the real challenge lies in how you act, on a day-to-day basis, when you get there. After all, when you're addressing the court, you're the centre of attention. You're talking, and people are (hopefully) listening. It's all about you, except that it isn't. It's about your client, and you representing them, and their interests, in a situation which is potentially as stressful for them as anything else that they will do in their life, even though, to you, it's literally just another day at the coalface. They have waited months, if not years, for this moment in court. They have spent that time worrying about the case, looking for documents, poring over evidence, stressing about dealing with solicitors, and then, often at the last minute, they're told that the case is going to be handed over to a barrister for the final push over the line.

When do they meet that barrister? On the morning of the hearing. When did the barrister get the papers? The night before. How can that barrister suddenly become au fait with matters which have taken years to distil to this point? How can they trust you to win the case when, for you, it's just one of many, whilst for them it is everything?

**Practice:**
The quick answer is: Prepare. Just prepare. Read that case as if your life depends on it. Think about what you need to prove, and what the other side is going to be trying to achieve. How are you going to thwart their efforts? How are you going to thwart their thwarting. Set out your end-points and decide how you want to get there.

Then breathe. Put yourself in their shoes. See yourself as they might see you. How are you going to present to them? Critically, try to understand just what they have invested in their case, and the trust that they are going to have put in you. By stopping and thinking about that, you will give yourself the chance to appreciate your importance rather than your self-importance, and that will make a real difference.

**Your notes:**
Why is our client involved in this litigation?

What is our client trying to achieve?

Why have I been instructed?

What I am trying to achieve?

If my aims and expectations are different from those of my client, why is that? Which are more realistic?

Do I need to sell those potential end-points to the client in advance? How am I going to do that?

How do I do the best for the client?

Why is our client involved in this litigation?

What is our client trying to achieve?

Why have I been instructed?

What I am trying to achieve?

If my aims and expectations are different from those of my client, why is that? Which are more realistic?

Do I need to sell those potential end-points to the client in advance? How am I going to do that?

How do I do the best for the client?

Why is our client involved in this litigation?

What is our client trying to achieve?

Why have I been instructed?

What I am trying to achieve?

If my aims and expectations are different from those of my client, why is that? Which are more realistic?

Do I need to sell those potential end-points to the client in advance? How am I going to do that?

How do I do the best for the client?

Why is our client involved in this litigation?

What is our client trying to achieve?

Why have I been instructed?

What I am trying to achieve?

If my aims and expectations are different from those of my client, why is that? Which are more realistic?

Do I need to sell those potential end-points to the client in advance? How am I going to do that?

How do I do the best for the client?

Why is our client involved in this litigation?

What is our client trying to achieve?

Why have I been instructed?

What I am trying to achieve?

If my aims and expectations are different from those of my client, why is that? Which are more realistic?

Do I need to sell those potential end-points to the client in advance? How am I going to do that?

How do I do the best for the client?

# CHAPTER TEN
## WHO TO IMPRESS

**The Monologue:**
When you go to court, who do you want to impress?
You want to impress the judge, obviously, because
that's how you hope to win your case. You want to
impress him with your written advocacy, your fierce
cross-examination, your erudite submissions and your
court presence. You want him to remember you next
time you appear in that court. You want him to trust
your submissions and to rate you.

You want to impress your lay client. They've
entrusted their case to you, and they're paying you,
and they need to know that you're going out of your
way to win the case for them. It's their day, but in the
great scheme of things, they're probably only ever
going to have one case. Nevertheless, you want them
to win, and you want them to have positive memories
of the barrister who represented them. The nicest
thing a client can say to you at the end of a case, win,
lose or draw, is: "I'm glad you were on my side." I
once had a little old lady say "You were magnificent"
which is quite nice too.

In fact, you want to impress the lay client on the
other side too. You want them to be jealous that
they've not got you representing them. You want

them to look at their barrister and resent the fact that they weren't quite as good as you.

And you want to impress your opponent. You may never have met them before, and might not ever meet them again, but if you do a good job, and you're against them again next week, they'll give you that respect, or fear you, which might give you an edge that you wouldn't otherwise have had. You might become very good friends with them, just as a result of having fought hard, and having worked together as necessary, to sort out the case. And bear in mind that they will go back to Chambers, or home, or to their solicitors, and talk about the person on the other side.

You want to impress your solicitor, because they've sent you that case. They might know your work already, and that's why they've chosen you, but if they're going to send you work on merit (and you'd like to think that that's their plan), you want to do a good job to get that work in the future.

Of course, you want to impress the solicitor instructing your opponent. They can send you work too. I once lost a case in such spectacular fashion that the solicitor on the other side, watching the judge make unexpected findings of fact to pre-emptively nullify my carefully crafted submissions on the law, felt so sorry for me, and was so impressed with the fight that I put up, that he started instructing me himself and did so for many years.

Those are the obvious ones, but you should also look to impress the clerk, and the usher. If you get on well with the clerk, they'll tell you about the judge, what they're like, whether they're in a good mood today, whether you can email that skeleton to a specific email address to get it printed off without being charged for it in the court office. They might even make you a cup of coffee whilst you're waiting for the judge.

The usher, by the way, can do some of that too, but is particularly useful when you've got a busy list, and people are jostling for position. Do you want to get on and get gone? Do you want to avoid that particular judge and get yourself pushed down the list in the hope of drawing a longer straw? The usher who knows you, or is impressed by you, can be your best friend.

Finally, there's you. All that prep last night was to avoid looking foolish. You came up with that line of cross-examination, or submission. You had a case to present, which may or may not have been a winner.

Often there's very little that you can say or do to make a difference: the die has been cast before you even receive the papers, but sometimes you won a case that could have been lost, and that feeling is one of the best things about this job. So set out to impress yourself, so that you can look yourself in the mirror and be proud of what you've achieved.

**The Analysis:**
This takes those aspects we considered in the previous chapter into the wider picture. Importantly, there is no one correct answer, not least because you have so many different potential audiences, each with a different perception of your role, your personality, your performance. This chapter is about highlighting the need for you to think about all of those people, not to give you a cure-all, and the main part of this lesson comes in how you address it in practice.

**Practice:**
You are at the very early stages of your professional development. You may not have met a barrister before. You may be on your first mini-pupillage. You have no idea what to expect, you're stepping into the great unknown, you're nervous, and don't want to put a foot wrong. You already understand that you're hoping to make a good impression – we'd hope that

nobody sets out to make a bad impression. With that in mind, let's address the dos and don'ts of work experience and mini-pupillage, so that you get the most out of it, without blowing your chances for the future.

The basic rules and guidance that follow are not going to apply to every individual, every set of chambers or every situation, but will hopefully give you a real steer in practice. I leave you to make your own notes about how you might approach them.

1.  It's much easier to make a really bad impression than it is to make a really good one.

2.  The barrister or solicitor that you're shadowing is not being paid to look after you, to teach you or to train you. They are doing their day job with all of its pressures and stresses, and they are allowing you to tag along. Please don't expect too much from them. They've probably got enough on their plate. The same applies to everyone else in the room, including the client.

3.  As a lawyer, you are selling services, not goods. We're talking about time, knowledge, intellect, experience, persona, professionalism, enthusiasm

and work ethic. Here and now, as a mini-pupil, however well you've done to date within your cohort, you are coming to learn, not sell yourself. If you get the chance to sell yourself whilst learning, that's fine, but if you try to sell rather than learn, you're likely to get short shrift (see rule 1).

4.   The best way to make a good impression is by being sensible and professional, and, when you are offered the chance, showing that you understand that. In other words, play it safe, but try to do it well.

5.   The best way of making a bad impression is pretty much everything else. That's not massively helpful, so here's a list of dos and don'ts.

6.   Do some preparation. Look at the chambers' website, not so that you can regurgitate the facts of the case that John Smith did last week, but because it will give you a feel for what's going on. You don't need to use that information, but you should have it to hand.

7. Do dress the part if you can. The reality is that the Bar is still a very conservative profession. Barristers wear suits, particularly if they are going to court or meeting clients. Some chambers have a more relaxed dress code for members who are simply coming in to work at their desk, but you're trying to make the right impression whilst fading into the background. That's unlikely to happen if you decide to wear the translucent top, a cravat, that Peruvian woolly jumper you picked up during your gap year or the mid-thigh white party frock with the red roses all over it[1]. Put yourself in the client's position: you're in an important meeting and you're being asked to allow someone else to sit in. If they're not part of the professional set up, why would you let them sit in?

That said, and this is an important point, there are those who would love to come to the Bar who are intimidated by the tradition and the formality. They might not have a suit to wear, or a new pair of shoes. They might worry that they need to wear a three-piece suit, or speak in a certain way. They might worry that they didn't go to the right university or that they'll be asked

---

1   And for those thinking that would never happen, they have.

a difficult question and look foolish. That fear of looking foolish can be paralysing.

If that's you, don't worry. Start with the basics. If you've got a straight choice between a dark suit and a light suit, wear the dark one. If you've got the choice between the patterned outfit and the plain outfit, wear the plain one. Plain mid-grey or patterned black? Probably the plain. If you've got the choice between a white shirt/blouse/top and anything else, wear a white one. If you can polish your shoes beforehand, do it – it's a small point, but people will notice if you look like you've been walking through a muddy field. Do up the top button of your plain white shirt and wear a simple tie, preferably not tied slackly, 3 inches below your open top button. Dress so that the client might imagine that you're a barrister in waiting. In effect, you are.

If you haven't got a suit, try to wear a dark jacket. Again, you're trying to be a fly on the wall and nothing more. If in doubt, keep to black (or charcoal, dark blue or grey) and white. Given the choice between what you might wear for a funeral and what you might wear for a wedding, or a Friday night out, you're safer going for the funereal outfit.

If in doubt, please, please ask. Ring up the week before and ask the receptionist, or a clerk, if there's a specific dress code. If you're making the effort to ask, they'll make the effort to help you, and you'll get credit for your openness and willingness to learn.

8. Turn up on time, and if you're running late, or can't make it, ring up and apologise. Keeping people in the loop is a huge part of professional life, and simply not turning up is unforgivable when people are putting themselves out to accommodate you.

9. Bring a notebook (maybe this book) and a pen, but ask if it's ok to take notes in conference before you do. Don't doodle.

10. Put your phone on silent, or better still, switch it off. If you need it at any point, you can switch it on, but your focus has to be on what is going on in front of you, not the rest of the world.

11. Be nice to the reception staff and clerks. They're far more important than you might think.

12. When you get to chambers, look to see where the toilets are (or ask at reception): chances are that you'll use them at some point during your visit, preferably not in the middle of a conference.

13. Good manners cost nothing (as I was taught as a child). If you're meeting clients, wait to be introduced, stand up when someone (particularly your client) comes into the room, offer to pour the tea, and try not to fall asleep, no matter how boring you might be finding proceedings.

14. When meeting a barrister, and wondering what to call them, go with Mr Smith or Miss Jones rather than first names. If they want you to use their first name, they'll tell you[2]. If you're in front of a client, revert to Mr Smith or Miss Jones, even if the client is calling the barrister by the first name.

---

2    Don't ever shorten their name to a diminutive, no matter what the circumstances. Call me 'Dave' and I'll break your fingers.

15. In conference, don't speak unless spoken to, and never, ever, opine on the case unless asked by the barrister. If the client asks you what you'd do in their position, you politely explain that you're only here to observe and learn, and that you're very sorry but you can't offer an opinion.

16. If you believe that the barrister has made a mistake in the advice being given, do not jump in and say so. Either they've not, in which case you annoy everybody, or they have, in which case they don't need to be embarrassed in front of the client. If you're sure, wait for a convenient moment, ask if you might ask a question, and then, respectfully and preferably outside earshot of the solicitor and client, ask whether your understanding was correct because you recalled the recent case of *Smith* which you'd understood to say something slightly different. Even if you're right, if you jump in you're unlikely to get any credit for it.

17. If you're speaking with the barrister socially, over lunch or otherwise, perhaps if the client has gone but the solicitor remains, let them lead the conversation and keep it work-related if you can. You may feel very strongly about the political

issues of the day, or have something else that you want to get off your chest, but the chances are that you're better using your time in chambers or in court learning about being in chambers or court.

18. Be aware that if you're going to court, they will expect to search your bag, and if you've got a bottle of perfume in there, or your overnight bag[3] you'll have to hand things over to security, causing delays etc. If in doubt, leave it at home, or in chambers.

19. If you're moving in court when a witness is taking the oath, stop and let them finish it. It's an important part of their evidence, and a judge will not be impressed if you get up to nip to the toilet.

20. If in doubt, take your lead from what others are doing, and then dial it back down a bit (or a lot). There are so many variables that no list can be exhaustive, but there is never a good side to trying to out-do the barrister with whom you're

---

3  I forgot to reclaim my nice razor from Portsmouth County Court.

spending time. Never feel pressurised into doing something that you're not comfortable with, just because you think it will please your host. Your mini-pupillage placement is loosely based on office hours (a conference can always overrun) so you shouldn't be heading off to the pub with them at 6pm, no matter that you've been invited. Make an excuse and go home.

21. Go away at the end of the day and write up your notes for future reference, revisiting chapter 1.

22. Don't post details of everything that you've seen on social media. In fact, look at your social media before you decide to apply for mini-pupillage and either lock down your privacy settings or think about whether that's the professional persona that you want chambers to see.

23. Always feel free to thank people for their time. You don't need to send gifts and promise undying loyalty: a simple email or letter will stand you in much better stead.

24. Make the most of it – there are dozens of others who'd love to be in your shoes.

**Your notes:**

## CHAPTER ELEVEN
## NOT WORTH IT

**The Monologue:**
My hourly rate is £x per hour, plus VAT. That means that if I'm meeting a client for, say, an hour and a half, with preparation time, the bill – the nominal cost to the client – could easily run to £1,000 or more. For some clients, that could be four, five, even six weeks of benefits or income. For an hour and half of my time. Six weeks' earnings.

And. I'm. Not. Worth. It.

Nobody is. I refuse to accept that. Six weeks income to spend 90 minutes with somebody? That's nonsense.

But I will strive to be worth it. I will do my damnedest to be worth it. I will treat them with respect. I will make sure that they get the best chocolate biscuits, rather than generic rich teas. I will walk them back to their car with an umbrella if it's raining. I will try to make their day. Because then and only then can I look myself in the mirror.

**The Analysis:**
Whilst the look on a mini-pupil's face when I deliver chapter 7 (*"I don't know"*) is often one of curiosity,

realisation and then wonder, this lesson normally gives rise to straight incredulity. Why would somebody charging so much for their time do such little things?

Part of the answer is, of course, that we can. We are in a privileged position. One benefit of being self-employed is that you don't have to account for that 30 second walk to the car. The cost of better biscuits is very modest, and the look on your child client's face when he's had a biscuit and half a fruit platter and you ask him if he'd like to take the rest home for his little brother makes you happy. We know the advertising slogan: the cost was this much, the outcome priceless.

We sell our time and our expertise. We can make a huge difference to people's lives. We can hold their freedom in our hands. There's really no point in being anything other than the best person that you can be. You don't have to, of course. You don't have to put yourself out at all, but it comes back to the fact that it's easier to make a bad impression than a good one.

If you strive to be as good as you can be, you will think of better ways to achieve those goals. You will try to improve little things which have a knock-on effect on everything else that you do. You become better and your clients might actually believe that you are offering them a commodity worth having.

If, on the other hand, you see yourself as entitled to charge whatever your hourly rate might be, you won't work for it and you won't try to improve. And that begs the question: If anybody could do this job and make the money that some barristers can, why doesn't everybody do it? And if anybody can do it, why should we pay the fees we do?

There are, to my mind, two types of barrister: spare mouths, and spare brains. Neither is better than the other. Some cases simply require a messenger to deliver a straight-forward message to the court. Some cases require a fresh pair of eyes to take the next step, or to understand where the end point might be. There are hugely successful spare mouth barristers, and I'd like to think of many of them as my friends. They have an astonishing work ethic and ability to process a certain type of information. They are handsomely paid for it, because they can process a huge volume of work. They have found their niche, and have loyal solicitors who will send them work for as long as that work exists, but that work is not immune to attack: a standard fee can be reduced arbitrarily by the Rules Committee, and the volume of work can be reduced by a change in the parameters which allow for claims to be made.

The spare brain is a different beast. It won't be as efficient in its billing. An hourly rate rather than a piece rate can be hard taskmaster. You can spend hours wading through documents looking for an answer that isn't there.[1]

The Bar is still under attack. Solicitors want to take our 'easy' work because they see it as a way to make a profit. They want the swings, whilst we get the roundabouts. There is a media narrative of the Bar as an old-fashioned, insular, privileged, elite. There is a government narrative that too much money is spent

---

1   I once spent 2½ days trying to find an answer to a problem, caused by the parties not having complied with the standard rules that should have been applied to a situation. Eventually I located a 200 year-old authority which won the case. At assessment of our costs, the other side took the point that the fee was unreasonable, because 'everyone knows that you can't bring an action in these circumstances, and it would only take an hour and a half to write an advice to that effect', entirely missing the point that the reason they were being asked to pay those costs was because I'd had the temerity to prove them wrong.

on law. There are financial pressures which make efficiency ever more important.

This is not an easy job. For me, and thousands like me, it is not just a job, or a career, or even a vocation. It is a way of life that brings both pleasure and pressure. If it is for you, it is a wonderful way to spend your time, with camaraderie and satisfaction to be had in equal measure. If it is not for you, then there is no shame in that, but you cannot realistically do what a barrister does without being committed to being the best you can be. So strive.

**Practice:**
In many ways, this chapter speaks for itself, but a simple thing to do is this: At the end of each day of your mini-pupillage or work experience placement, try to write down three things.

1. Something you saw somebody do that you liked that you wouldn't have thought to do yourself but would do in the future.

2. Something you saw somebody do that you didn't like and would have done differently, together with your reasons why.

3.   Something you saw that you didn't understand.
     It might be that you get the chance to ask why
     that person did what they did. It may be that it
     becomes important at some point in the future.

The notes section below is simply divided up into
those three sections, each with a double page for you
to fill.

**Your notes:**
What would I add to my repertoire?

What would I add to my repertoire?

What would I try not to do and how might I do it instead?

What would I try not to do and how might I do it instead?

What did I see that I need to go away and think about?

What did I see that I need to go away and think about?

# CHAPTER TWELVE
## FORENSIC INTENSITY

**The Monologue:**
Balance forensic intensity with calm self-awareness.

**The Analysis:**
Having been asked time and time again for advice as to how to get a scholarship, or a pupillage interview, or pupillage, or tenancy, or something, this is the answer.

There is no one identikit barrister. It is a profession that is open to those who are good enough. It is hugely over-subscribed, and it is expensive to train, particularly when there is no guarantee that you will reach the next stage. Scholarships are particularly prized as a means to avoid that particular tranche of student debt which weighs you down at the start of your career. Much has been written about the profile of the Bar, perhaps more so than other professions, and much work has been done to improve accessibility. The pool of candidates is wider than ever, but that increase in numbers increases the competition for all, and the best advice has, therefore, to be personal to the individual candidate. Balance forensic intensity with calm self-awareness. Be good. Don't be a prat.

The first part is, in many ways, obvious. If you want a scholarship, you need to be worthy of it. That's not for you to decide, but the person making the offer. If you don't ask, you don't get, and you shouldn't not apply, just because you don't think you're good enough.

'Forensic intensity' is an unusual phrase, and yet to those at the Bar it is absolutely transparent. It's not about shouting at people. It's about being focused on what you're trying to achieve and how you're going to achieve it. It really is as simple as that. Strip out the chaff. Focus on the real issues in the case, in your practice, in your life. Analyse the details, and be able to step into the evidence, but remember to step back from time to time to make sure that your overview is how you remember it. Never be afraid just to stop for a second and think. Let the evidential maelstrom move on a little, just to give you the space to observe the storm before plunging back in.

Equally, though, there are people who think that they would like to be a barrister who will struggle to achieve their goals. That is the reality of life: there are always things that we cannot do.

Having an understanding of how good you actually are is just as important as your objective standard. If you're a 7/10, but you think that you're a 5, you'll never push yourself. If you think that you're a 10, you can over-reach and fail. Understand that you're a 7/10, but would like to make it to an 8, and you can take those steps, establish yourself as an 8, and then look to see whether you can push to a 9.

Having those internal checks and balances is a hugely important part of being a barrister. The trainee solicitor can seek assistance from their supervisor. The supervisor can seek assistance from a partner in the firm. The partner can seek assistance from a barrister. Each in turn can reach up the forensic chain for a second opinion, or advice, or just confirmation that what they are doing is right.

As a barrister, it is far less clear cut. You might be able to ask advice from somebody else in chambers, a friend, your pupil supervisor, another barrister at court, but often the buck stops with you. There is no safety net, and if the question was easy, you wouldn't have been asked, would you?

Understanding your limitations is a critical part of being a barrister. There's a huge pressure, particularly when you are starting out, to take on every piece of work and every type of work. Often that will be beyond your competence. Knowing what you can and can't do, and when to say no, is a key attribute. Push too hard and you'll get into trouble. Don't push, and you'll never learn anything.

That's the self-awareness issue, but why 'calm'?

In simple terms, there's no point in not being calm. Objectivity requires some sense of distance, no matter how small, and if you forget to breathe, forget to stop, forget to think, you get so bound up in the problem that it's impossible to be objective.

Understanding that you cannot know everything, that you cannot understand everything, that you cannot control everything and that you cannot win everything is a fundamental tenet of what we do. Accepting that is not easy.

You need to have judgment, and that is something that you cannot simply be taught. It is something that you develop over time, with insight. Maintaining progress whilst simultaneously maintaining control is far from easy, but is a skill well worth developing.

I started this book with a reference to one of my chess heroes, David Bronstein. I finish it with reference to another, Alexander Alexandrovich Alekhine[1], a man described as having "a special ability to provoke complications without taking excessive risks".

Alekhine said that 'Chess is not only knowledge and logic.'

The same applies to legal practice.

**Practice:**
Balance forensic intensity with calm self-awareness.

Be good. Don't be a prat.

---

1    1892-1946, World Chess Champion 1927-1935, 1935-1946

**Your notes:**

# PRAISE FOR ON EXPERTS

"He writes as he speaks: He surveys the territory with the advantage of a wealth of experience, richly leavened with a generous helping of personal anecdote, thereby combining authority with accessibility."
– Turner J

"A well-written, comprehensive and engaging account of the issues encountered in being a medical expert … clearly important and worthy of wider dissemination"
– Professor Hector Chinoy, PhD FRCP, Senior Lecturer & Honorary Consultant Rheumatologist

"Clearly informed by extensive practical experience … this is a book that is needed and should be purchased by lawyers and anyone who is thinking of giving 'expert' evidence"
– Gordon Exall, Barrister

"Eloquently explains a number of complex issues relating to pitfalls in civil expert evidence … all experts will benefit from the contents of this book"
– Peter Etherington, Forensic Engineer

"Should be used as a teaching guide for new judges, let alone Counsel, litigation solicitors and experts"
– Timothy Gray, District Judge

# PRAISE FOR AN INTRODUCTION TO PERSONAL INJURY LAW

"A very fine over-view of this important area … explaining in lucid terms, to professional and lay clients alike, the relevant underlying principles and the practical nuts and bolts of personal injury law… a splendid vade mecum for those seeking a true introduction to this field."
– Stewart J

"A comprehensive, easy to read, guide to personal injury claims with a wealth of information to assist even the most experienced practitioner."
– Lesley Graham, Past President, CILEx

"In this impressive yet concise work, the author has successfully achieved the ambitious twin aims of clearly communicating practical knowledge drawn from specialist experience, and conveying to the reader a wider understanding of the broader issues and drivers of behaviour in personal injury disputes. Doing so with an accessible style and pragmatic approach is a real achievement. I have no doubt that this work will soon become an immensely valuable go-to resource for anyone needing to understand quickly the important issues in this complex field."
– John Bates, Senior Tort Lecturer, Northumbria University

# ABOUT THE AUTHOR

With A-levels in Maths, Physics and Chemistry from the Manchester Grammar School, David Boyle read Law at Churchill College, Cambridge where he spent his time narrowly failing to be picked for the Varsity Chess team, or the College First VIII, XI or XV.

After Bar School in London, he returned to Manchester in 1995 where he undertook pupillage at Deans Court Chambers under the supervision of HHJ Craig Sephton QC (as he now is).

He is a specialist personal injury practitioner, working for both claimants and defendants, and is a first port of call for 'interesting' cases having represented peers of the realm and professional footballers, and having sued the Health & Safety Executive and the Federal Republic of Nigeria.

From 2010 to 2016 he was head of mini-pupillage at Deans Court, instigating their 'Mini-Pupillage Day' event and the dreaded (and now retired) Homework™ where MPs tried to describe a photograph in 250 words. His (frankly visceral) feedback was once described as "Beyond distressing, but the best I've ever had."

He has lectured, spoken, and written on countless subjects, to audiences from primary school children through to medical consultants.

In 2019, he was the first civil barrister appointed to the Bar Standard Board's Advisory Panel of Experts.

His first book, On Experts, was the first of its type, aimed at both lawyers and experts alike, but accessible to the layman.

His second book, An Introduction to Personal Injury Law, has become a mainstay for established non-PI practitioners who need a swift, effective grounding in that area of law.

What was to have been his next volume, Case Management, is currently under a dust sheet, having given way to this, his third book.

Everything in this book is true to the best of his knowledge and belief, particularly the Author's Note.